CAN YOU IMAGINE?

Being a TOUCAN

By Katherine Ponka

Gareth Stevens
Publishing

Please visit our website, www.garethstevens.com. For a free color catalog of all our high-quality books, call toll free 1-800-542-2595 or fax 1-877-542-2596.

Library of Congress Cataloging-in-Publication Data

Ponka, Katherine E.
Being a toucan / by Katherine E. Ponka.
  p. cm. — (Can you imagine?)
Includes index.
ISBN 978-1-4824-3280-0 (pbk.)
ISBN 978-1-4824-0131-8 (6-pack)
ISBN 978-1-4824-0130-1 (library binding)
1. Toucans — Juvenile literature. I. Title.
QL696.P57 P66 2014
598.72—dc23

First Edition

Published in 2014 by
Gareth Stevens Publishing
111 East 14th Street, Suite 349
New York, NY 10003

Copyright © 2014 Gareth Stevens Publishing

Designer: Katelyn E. Reynolds
Editor: Therese Shea

Photo credits: Cover, pp. 1, 9 (inset) Eduardo Rivero/Shutterstock.com; cover, pp. 1–32 (background texture) AnnabelleaDesigns/Shutterstock.com; p. 5 (diagram) Carlyn Iverson/Photo Researchers/Getty Images; p. 5 (photo) Urca Humaita/AFP/Getty Images; p. 7 Hemera/Thinkstock.com; p. 9 (main) Ralf Hettler/E+/Getty Images; p. 11 Yenyu Shih/Shutterstock.com; pp. 13, 19, 21 iStockphoto/Thinkstock.com; p. 14 wong yu liang/Shutterstock.com; pp. 15, 17 Visuals Unlimited, Inc./Gregory Basco/Getty Images; p. 18 De Agnostini Picture Library/Getty Images; p. 22 Ekaterina V. Borisova/Shutterstock.com; p. 23 Daniel Novak/Flickr/Getty Images; p. 24 Cyril Laubscher/Dorling Kindersley/Getty Images; p. 25 Tatiane Noviski Fornel/Flickr/Getty Images; p. 27 ariadna de raadt/Shutterstock.com; p. 28 DDCoral/Shutterstock.com; p. 29 moaan/Flickr/Getty Images.

Printed in the United States of America

CPSIA compliance information: Batch #CW14GS: For further information contact Gareth Stevens, New York, New York at 1-800-542-2595.

CONTENTS

Words in the glossary appear in **bold** type the first time they are used in the text.

THE CANOPY

Picture yourself walking through a wet, green forest. It's very hot, and water drips off the leaves from yet another rainfall. This forest is called a **tropical** rainforest. More than half of all plants and animals on the planet live in rainforests.

There are four layers in a rainforest. The second layer from the top is called the canopy. There, the overlapping leaves and branches can be 100 feet (30 m) above the forest floor. And yet, many colorful creatures are found in the canopy.

The emergent layer contains the very tops of the tallest trees. The canopy forms a roof over the rainforest. The understory has young trees and shrubs, and the forest floor is home to ground plants and animals.

The Layers of the Rainforest

emergent layer

canopy layer

understory layer

forest floor

HOT HOME

The canopy is drier and gets more sunlight than the understory and forest floor. The many animals that live in the canopy like this kind of **habitat**. The rainforest canopies of Central and South America are home to the colorful birds called toucans.

Toucans have a very large, multicolored **bill** and often have feathers with bright colors. They mostly stay in the rainforest canopy their whole lives. Do you think you'd like to be this fun bird? Read on to find out more.

imagine that!

Toucans hardly ever leave the tops of the trees to walk on the ground.

Besides rainforests, toucans live in more open forests and in **savannas**.

Central America

South America

☐ toucan range

BIGGEST AND SMALLEST

So far, 41 different kinds, or species, of toucans have been counted. The largest and heaviest toucan is the toco toucan. It can be 24 inches (61 cm) long and weigh about 1.9 pounds (0.9 kg). Male toco toucans are a bit larger than females.

The lightest toucan, the lettered aracari, is just 3.4 ounces (96 g). The smallest toucan, the tawny-tufted toucanet, is just over a foot (30 cm) long—not too small! Which toucan species would you like to be?

imagine that!

Aracaris and toucanets have different names but are still toucans.

toco toucan

All toucans are mostly black with a different-colored throat and a long bill.

collared aracari

9

WOW!
WHAT A BILL!

Imagine if your nose were one-third the size of your body! That's how big a toucan's bill is. The toco toucan's bill can be 7.5 inches (19 cm) long. It's a good tool for reaching food from a distance!

Have you ever seen a honeycomb? The inside of a toucan's bill looks like one. A toucan's bill is made of **keratin** arranged in a honeycomb pattern. The bill has toothlike edges that help a toucan grab and even skin its food.

imagine that!

The ancient Aztecs believed that the toucan's bill was created from rainbows. It was the toucan's reward for being a messenger of the gods.

Toucans don't have a strong bite. They need their special bill to help them eat.

RAINFOREST FOOD

If you were a toucan, you wouldn't **migrate** like many other birds do. You'd have plenty to eat in the rainforest canopy all year. You'd love fruits and berries. Your large toucan bill would come in handy to smash soft fruit as well as to skin tougher fruit. And you might also eat bugs, lizards, eggs, and even baby birds!

Toucans play an important role in the forest. They eat fruit seeds and help spread them throughout the rainforest. These seeds grow into new fruit trees.

imagine that!

Toucans can fly but not that well. They mostly hop from tree to tree.

Toucans are mainly frugivorous (froo-JIH-vuh-ruhs). That means they mostly eat fruit.

13

EATING, TOUCAN-STYLE

If you were a toucan, you might pick up a bit of food with the tip of your bill and throw it up in the air. Then, you'd open wide and let the food just fall into your mouth!

Toucans have a long, thin tongue that has edges like a feather. All these edges help a toucan taste. The tongue also helps the toucan catch food and get tiny pieces down its long bill and into its throat.

imagine that!

The keel-billed toucan is the national bird of Belize, a country in Central America.

Do you think you could eat your food like this keel-billed toucan?

15

TOUCAN TOGETHERNESS

If you were a toucan, you'd make your nest in a tree hollow. You might live with friends, too. Toucans live in pairs or flocks. Sometimes, several toucans live in one small hole. It gets crowded!

Female toucans lay one to five shiny white eggs once a year in the spring. Their nests aren't lined with much, perhaps a few wood chips and some seeds. Both toucan parents take turns sitting on the eggs. Toucan eggs hatch in a little over 2 weeks.

imagine that!

A nest of toucan eggs is called a clutch.

This chestnut-mandibled toucan fits snugly into a tree hollow. Sometimes, toucans take over hollows made by other animals, such as woodpeckers.

17

CHICKS

If you were a newly hatched toucan, you'd have no feathers at first, and your eyes would be closed. You'd have pads on your heels to protect your feet from the rough floor of the nest. Toucan chicks begin to get small fluffy feathers after about 3 weeks. They stay in the nest up to 8 weeks, getting food from their parents.

Chicks have a small bill. The bill doesn't reach its full size until a chick is several months old.

Though they don't have a big bill yet, these toucan chicks have already grown some bright feathers.

HIDING IN PLAIN SIGHT

If you were a toucan, you'd be hunted by large **carnivorous** birds, jaguars, and snakes! You might think that a toucan's body would stand out in the rainforest. However, its bright feathers and beak actually blend in with tropical fruits and flowers, like **camouflage**! Its black and white feathers look like the patches of sunlight and shadow in the trees.

Scientists think the bird's big bill is also meant to scare away predators. However, toucans don't use their bills to fight.

imagine that!

Toucans are related to the woodpecker.

A toucan's many colors help it hide from predators.

ON THE PERCH

If you were a toucan getting ready to sleep at night, you'd turn your head all the way around and rest your bill on your back. Your tail would fold up over your body. With your feet firmly **clamped** on the branch, you'd look like one large ball of feathers!

Toucan toes give them strength to grip their **perch** tightly whether they're eating or sleeping. The four toes on each foot are in pairs, with the first and fourth toes curled back.

Toucans sleep in some unusual positions. This may be so they can sleep in tight spaces, like tree hollows.

23

SPLISH SPLASH

If you were a toucan, you'd still take baths. There aren't any bathtubs in the rainforest, so you'd find something similar. Rainwater can pool in parts of trees. So, when you wanted to get clean, all you'd have to do is find one of these.

Toucans use their bills to clean their own feathers. They also help other toucans stay clean by picking bugs out of their feathers. The cleaning and smoothing of feathers is called preening.

As a toucan in the wild, you'd get most of the water you need in the fruits you eat.

PLAYING AND TALKING

If you were a toucan, you'd find time to play each day. You and another toucan might bang your bills as if you're sword fighting! You might also use your bill and a piece of fruit to play catch with a friend. Toucan **mates** toss each other fruit, too.

Toucans are quite **intelligent**. They may **clack** their bills as a kind of message. Toucans are loud talkers, too. They repeat croaking or rattling kinds of calls.

imagine that!

Toucans in the wild live about 20 years.

Remember, toucans can't bite hard. These birds are just playing.

27

TOUCANS AS PETS

If you were a toucan, lots of people would love to have you as a pet! People pay a lot of money to own toucans. It costs a lot to feed and take care of a toucan as well. Toucans need big, airy cages.

Toucans can be quite friendly. They like to be scratched and petted, and can even be trained to sit on your shoulder. Some happy toucans make purring sounds! Even if you don't want to be a toucan, would you want to own one?

If you were a toucan, you might live in a zoo so lots of people could visit you!

29

GLOSSARY

bill: the beak of a bird

camouflage: colors or shapes in animals that allow them to blend in with their surroundings

carnivorous: meat eating

clack: to make a short, hard, loud noise

clamp: to hold something tightly and firmly

habitat: the natural place where an animal or plant lives

intelligent: having the ability to learn skills and apply them

keratin: a hard substance making up hair, fingernails, horns, and hoofs

mate: one of two animals that come together to make babies

migrate: to move from one area to another for feeding or having babies

perch: a place for a bird to land or rest

savanna: a grassland with scattered patches of trees

tropical: having to do with the warm parts of Earth near the equator

FOR MORE INFORMATION

Books

Dunn, Mary R. *Toucans*. North Mankato, MN: Capstone Press, 2012.

Kite, Lorien. *Toucans*. Danbury, CT: Grolier, 2009.

Patkau, Karen. *Who Needs a Jungle? A Rainforest Ecosystem*. Toronto, ON: Tundra Books, 2012.

Websites

Birds: Toucan
animals.sandiegozoo.org/animals/toucan
Read many fun facts about the toucan.

Toucan
animals.nationalgeographic.com/animals/birds/toucan
Hear what a toucan sounds like.

INDEX